Buffalo

Nicole Boswell

The buffalo is a large animal.
It looks like a really big cow.

Buffaloes do not see or hear well, but they can smell well.

Buffaloes live close to water.

They live in groups called herds.

They like to eat grass.

They like to lie in the mud when it is hot.

horns

calf

nose

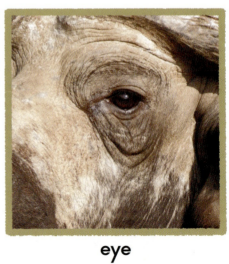
eye